COMMUNITY AND RACE RELATIONS TRAINING FOR THE POLICE

Report of the Police Training Council Working Party

Home Office
50 Queen Anne's Gate
LONDON
SW1H 9AT

February 1983

© Crown Copyright 1983

First published 1983

ISBN 0 86252 090 8 ✓

Printed for the Home Office by Her Majesty's Stationery Office

CONTENTS

APPENDICES

Note

The more important conclusions of this report are sidelined in the margin. The conclusions as a whole including proposals for community and race relations training in future, are summarised in paragraph 9.1.

REPORT OF THE POLICE TRAINING COUNCIL WORKING PARTY ON COMMUNITY AND RACE RELATIONS TRAINING FOR THE POLICE

INTRODUCTION

1.1 We were appointed by the Police Training Council in January 1982:

> "To review the community relations training given to the police, with particular reference to race relations training as mentioned in Lord Scarman's Report and taking account of the Home Secretary's Foreword to the report of the Racial Attacks study and to make recommendations."

1.2 Our membership is set out in Appendix 1. Besides representatives of the Police Service and other constituent bodies of the Police Training Council our membership has included a number of individuals from minority ethnic communities with experience of, and expertise in, police training. We believe that the multi-racial nature of our group has made an indispensable contribution to our work, and that the different perspectives and experience that members have been able to bring to bear have been an invaluable aid to our understanding of the difficult issues involved.

1.3 We have held seven meetings. To provide information about present arrangements for training in community and race relations we have had available to us the results of a questionnaire survey of all forces in England and Wales. We are grateful for the information that forces were able to provide. We should also like to put on record our thanks to Captain M J Marriott, the Director of the United States Navy Human Resources Management Programme and former Director of the United States' Department of Defence Equal Opportunity Management Institute at Patrick Air Force Base, Florida, who presented to us a model of training in race relations based on his long and first hand experience of the development of the arrangements that have been found to be necessary by the United States Military.

1.4 We are conscious that our work has proceeded in parallel with that of a quite separate Working Party appointed by the Police Training Council to examine the training given to probationer constables and of reviews, also being carried out under the aegis of the Council, of training in the handling of public disorder, and of supervision and management training. We have kept closely in touch with the progress made by these groups. It will fall to them to decide how best to incorporate future training in community and race relations into the training programmes they recommend. We accept that some minor adjustments to what we propose may in the event prove necessary, but we firmly believe that the principles and practice that we recommend should inform community and race relations training throughout the service and will be essential to its success.

TERMINOLOGY

1.5 Commentators on race relations often refer loosely to the "ethnic minorities". This description is generally meant to refer to all those communities in our society which are distinguished by their colour from the white majority population. In implying that white people belong to no ethnic group and that the rest of the population can be regarded as homogeneous the phrase is misleading and may be offensive. The different racial and ethnic groups which now compose our society are, however, too numerous to refer to individually in a report of this kind and some choice of terminology has been necessary. Throughout the report therefore we use the phrases "minority ethnic communities" or "minority ethnic groups" to refer to all those minority communities or groups which are distinguished by their colour from the ethnic majority.

1.6 We are, of course, aware that there is now a significant number of officers from the minority ethnic communities in the police service. The training we recommend is intended overall to be as suitable for them as for their colleagues from the ethnic majority and we have not sought to single them out in the text of our report. Readers will therefore need to bear in mind, unless it is otherwise clear from the context, that when we use the terms "police" or "officers" we mean to refer to police officers of both minority and majority ethnic origin.

THE CONTEXT OF OUR WORK

1.7 As our terms of reference make clear we began work following the publication in November 1981 of two reports. One was the Report of Lord Scarman's inquiry into the disorders in Brixton in April 1981.[1] Lord Scarman recognised that the initial training given to the police already includes an element of instruction in community relations but recommended that this should be strengthened. He went on to recommend (5.28) that:

> "Training courses designed to develop the understanding that good community relations are not merely necessary but essential to good policing should ..... be compulsory from time to time in a police officer's career up to and including the rank of Superintendent. The theme of these courses should be the role of the police as part of the community, the operational importance of good community relations, the techniques of consultation, and the moral as well as legal accountability of the police to the public."

1.8 The other report was of a Home Office study of the incidence of racial attacks and the activities of extremist organisations alleged to be responsible for them.[2] The report frankly recognised that racial attacks were a major and worrying source of friction and misunderstanding between the police and the minority ethnic communities. In the light of the study's findings, the Home Secretary announced that he wished to pursue a number of lines of action. Among these were:

> "training of police officers which will enable them to develop a greater sensitivity towards the phenomenon of racial attacks and their severe impact on minority communities – this training to be focussed on involvement in the community as much as in the classroom",

and

> "... assistance to the police by ethnic minority groups with on the job training for police officers."

1.9 The recommendations in these reports must, of course, be seen against the background of the difficulties which have marked relations between the police and the public in recent years. In our evolving society the exercise of authority, whether by the police or others is, personally and professionally, testing to the highest degree. The responsibilities the police bear on our behalf are difficult and onerous and cannot effectively be discharged even by the most skilful practitioners, without the support of the whole community. Training is an indispensable element in that support, and we have regarded it as our task to recommend training that will give individual police officers the practical help that they need and that society owes them.

1.10 Nowhere is this need for practical help greater than in race relations. It is a fact that racial prejudice and discrimination whether conscious or unconscious are widespread in this country. The police, as a part of our society, reflect its mores and habits of thought. We cannot gauge the extent to which the police service is racially prejudiced or to which its practices are discriminatory. But that prejudice and discrimination exist in the police service and where they do can have grave consequences not merely for the welfare of individuals but for the health of relations between the police and our minority ethnic communities, we have no doubt. To acknowledge that the police need better training in race relations than they have had in the past is neither to ignore the efforts that they have already made nor to single them out. Racial discrimination is a part of the fabric of life in this country and is an evil which all agencies and services have a duty to eradicate. It is rather that until the reality of discrimination is faced honestly and squarely the problems cannot be effectively tackled. We have worked with this reality firmly in view and are clear that to be effective training must do the same.

1.11 Finally, training in community and race relations cannot be approached in isolation. It is essential that it should be viewed in the context of, in the first instance, policies for recruitment and secondly, of the acquisition of good management skills. The right officers must be recruited and their seniors trained to provide proper supervision and themselves to set an example.

---

1 The Brixton Disorders 10 - 12 April 1981 Cmnd 8427

2 Racial Attacks, Report of a Home Office Study, Home Office November 1981

SOME PRELIMINARY QUESTIONS

2.1 Before we turn to more substantive issues it may be useful to indicate where we stand on one or two preliminary questions.

2.2 We were asked to pay particular attention to race relations training but to deal also with community relations training across the board. In line with our terms of reference we have concentrated our efforts on deciding what improvements in race relations training are desirable for the future. Community relations training has, however, provided the overall context of our work. In the light of this we have asked ourselves whether race relations training can or should be regarded as one, albeit important, aspect of community relations training in general, or whether separate training is needed.

2.3 There is no doubt that race and community relations training go hand in hand. The requirements of good community relations are also the requirements of good race relations; and it is clear to us that many of the skills which police officers require in their dealings with members of minority ethnic groups will be invaluable in their encounters with the public at large. There are, therefore, good reasons for teaching race and community relations together. Such an approach would also help to avoid the danger, which we acknowledge, that by treating race separately training might inadvertently perpetuate the notion that our minority ethnic communities constitute simply another "problem" group for the police, or are somehow being specially favoured.

2.4 Nevertheless, it is important that race relations training should be accorded the special attention that it deserves. It is not simply that the most difficult and intractable problems between the police and the public arise where race is an issue; it is rather that racial and cultural differences can introduce complexities of a special nature and order into encounters between individuals and groups. We are concerned that those additional complexities should not be forgotten and that race relations should not be dealt with *simply* as a species of human relations. To ensure that race relations is given due weight we recommend that some time should consciously be set aside in programmes devoted to community relations for instruction focussed *specifically* on race relations. We recognise that the amount of time that will need to be devoted to race and community relations respectively will probably vary from force to force, and for this reason we make no recommendations as to how forces should apportion the training resources available to them. The general principle should, however, be that the needs of officers for training determine the time to be made available and *not* an arbitrary time allocated within which what is possible is fitted. We make clear below our belief that *all* police officers should receive a common core of training in race relations. For the moment we would only observe that in our view forces would be unwise to divide the time available in simple relation to the proportionate size of the minority ethnic population in their area. Serious tensions can arise even where there is only a small minority ethnic community.

2.5 We believe it right, too, to state at this stage where we stand on the question of whether training should seek to influence attitudes or behaviour. It is often assumed that race relations training should aim to ensure that the attitudes of individuals towards persons of a different race are tolerant and sympathetic. Others feel it is unsound, and can be counterproductive, to seek to modify attitudes and that the focus of training should be on the overt behaviour desired.

2.6 In our view it is misleading to suggest that these two strategies are incompatible and we recommend that both should have a place in future training programmes. So far as race relations are concerned attitudes are in an important sense at the heart of the matter. But attitude training will, we believe, only be of value to the police service if it goes together with the teaching of effective policing skills. On the other hand, while we recognise that in the final analysis what matters most to members of the public is that they should be treated in a correct and professional manner, it does not seem to us wise to rely entirely on the capacity of the well "trained" officer to mask his private attitudes. Our fear is that it is precisely under conditions of stress, and in circumstances where the benefits of adequate training are most needed, that unacceptable attitudes are likely to emerge.

THE REQUIREMENT FOR POLICE TRAINING IN COMMUNITY AND RACE RELATIONS

3.1 In addressing the need for training in community and race relations we have had in mind both the nature of policing and the qualities required by individual officers. Three points are of particular importance to training. First, a police officer fulfils many functions besides enforcing the law: he must also keep the peace, and, as is now known from research, what might be termed his "service" or non-enforcement role will generally account for a good deal more than half his time. These functions are no less his duty than enforcing the law and may have a profound effect on the respect with which he is viewed by the public he serves. Second, police work by its very nature involves the exercise of discretion. Third, for a mixture of moral and prudential reasons the *manner* in which the officer carries out his duty is of paramount importance. He must command respect; be firm but never authoritarian; be tactful and sensitive where necessary and treat all members of the public regardless of their race with unfailing patience, politeness and understanding.

3.2 In the light of these points we suggest that the basic need is for community and race relations training that in practice helps police officers to carry out their jobs effectively by giving them:

  a. an adequate conception of their various, and sometimes conflicting, roles and an appreciation of the part that each can play in cementing relations with the community;

  b. a full working knowledge of their local community; and

  c. the right attitude and skills to carry out their duties without giving unnecessary offence.

We deal very briefly with each of these requirements in turn below.

Roles

3.3 In practice much of an officer's time will be taken up with providing a diverse range of services, support, or aid to the public. Enforcing the law is a central function of the police service and it must not be forgotten that the success of the police in curbing crime is critical to their relations with the public. But so equally are the manner and enthusiasm with which officers discharge their service functions. Indeed, in some situations the other services provided by the police may be more critical. In the case of racial attacks, for example, where because of the nature of those offences the police are often unable to trace the offenders, the manner in which the victims are treated and the quality of the support which the police can provide will have a profound effect not merely on the individuals concerned but on relations between the police and the whole community from which the individual comes.

3 4 Many officers, of course, appreciate the need for the police to offer a full range of services and take pride in discharging all their functions in a thoughtful and professional manner. There is, however, a tendency for some, particularly in inner-city areas, to regard their task as more or less exclusively one of law enforcement. Such a narrow conception of their role can lead officers to exercise their discretion without regard to the effect of their actions on long-term relations with the public, and to regard themselves as representing an authority apart from the community. Officers who focus exclusively on law enforcement may, in addition, assume that all individuals with whom they come into contact are criminally inclined, and take a disparaging and moralistic view towards high crime areas (and the local populations) where the generally accepted means of social control may be relatively difficult to apply.

Knowledge of local community

3.5 A police officer needs more than a clear grasp of the law and the procedural framework within which he works. He must also be well and accurately informed about our multi-cultural society and the local community he serves. Without the necessary information police officers may misread the behaviour of members of the community and interpret with unnecessary suspicion the patterns of activity usual in it. They may enforce the law with insufficient

4

sensitivity to local conditions, react unduly defensively to different cultural attitudes to the authority they represent, or inadvertently offend the beliefs or customs of the community. At the very least a lack of the proper information may contribute to an unfortunate uncertainty in how to respond to incidents.

Attitudes and skills

3.6 In addition to a balanced conception of their role and an adequate grasp of the required information police officers need the skills and confidence accurately to assess the situations which confront them and to communicate effectively with the public. They need, for example, to be able to start and sustain a friendly conversation with strangers and to elicit the information they may require from the public without adopting an authoritarian manner. A lack of such skill or alternatively a lack of confidence will cause difficulties especially when the officer is dealing with people of a different race.

3.7 A lack of skill or confidence may affect officers' dealings with individuals regardless of his feelings towards them either as individuals or as members of a particular group. Their behaviour towards individuals or groups may, however, result not so much from any want of skills as from their fundamental attitudes. We have mentioned the particularly damaging consequences that racial prejudice may have, but other attitudes are also important in the relationship that officers are able to achieve with their public. A lack of proper professional impartiality or flexibility, for example, though perhaps lacking the potential ill-effects of racism may lead to contact with the public taking on undesirable overtones of personal conflict.

PRESENT ARRANGEMENTS FOR COMMUNITY AND RACE RELATIONS TRAINING FOR THE POLICE

4.1 In this section we describe the present arrangements for training and identify those areas where we feel the weaknesses lie.

4.2 Community and race relations training in provincial forces is given partly at the six regional recruit training centres run by the Home Office and partly in-force. So far as the *training given by the Home Office centres* is concerned roughly ten per cent of the initial course for recruits is taken up by what are called "associated police studies". Most of the topics taught under this head, for example, 'rights of the individual' are relevant to community and race relations to some degree. Two periods are set aside specifically for community relations and one further period is devoted to race relations. The training is given by means of lectures supported in some instances by films.

4.3 *In-force community and race relations training* is at the discretion of individual chief constables. So far as probationers are concerned forces were given some guidance in a circular issued by the Home Office in 1973, but the intention was that in-force race relations training in particular should be tailored to local needs. It is, therefore, no surprise that there is considerable variation in both the content and the amount of training provided by individual forces. A good deal of in-force training is under review and some forces are already taking steps to improve both the quality and quantity of the training in community and race relations which their officers receive. Our criticisms do not therefore apply equally to all training given in all forces. In the Metropolitan Police, principally, substantially new training in "human awareness" including training in race relations has been introduced for all recruits. To accommodate this new training the course has been extended by one week. Human awareness training is integrated with, and spread throughout the course.

4.4 We have approached our examination of present training not only in the light of our analysis of the needs which we have indicated (in section 3) training must seek to meet but with a number of other factors in mind. One of these is the findings of *research*. There is, unfortunately, no evidence available that will fully answer the question of what, if any, is the effect of the race and community relations training presently given to the police service in this country. Some useful work has, however, been done the results of which are, we believe, of importance and which have directly informed our criticisms of present training. Short notes prepared by the Home Office Research and Planning Unit on the studies drawn to our attention are at Appendix 2. The references do not provide a comprehensive list of research in the area under review, the intention being merely to illustrate the kind of evidence that has been produced; and we have drawn in the text of the report on the findings of individual studies without attribution.

4.5 Our approach has also been informed by the particular nature of community and race relations training. As we have made clear the need for training in these areas arises directly from the requirements of effective policing. Its fundamental aim must be to ensure that the *whole range* of police duties is carried out in a manner which is conducive to the maintenance of good relations with members of the public of all races. It is in our view important to recognise that in this sense while there are clearly some facts and skills that can conveniently be taught under the heading of "community and race relations" neither race nor community relations are *discrete* subjects on a par with, for example, traffic. They are aspects of all police work, and teaching in them cannot in principle therefore be wholly divorced from training in other topics. Some time must, it is clear, be devoted specifically to race and community relations; but to be fully effective *all* training in the police service must endeavour not just to teach the specific skills that are required for the effective discharge of the officers' duties in a particular area but also to draw out and reinforce those aspects of these skills which are of particular relevance and importance for community relations. With these points in mind we turn to our analysis of present training.

The extent and scope of present training

4.6 About four in every five forces give some training in community and race relations. We were concerned to discover, however, that six forces appear to give no training in community relations at all; and that in eight forces officers received no race relations training. Only a small number of forces clearly distinguish race from community relations training. Even where training is provided in those topics they are not accorded the priority they deserve. In about three-quarters of those forces which give some training in community and race relations, instruction is confined to one, two or three periods of 45 – 60 minutes. In the remaining quarter of forces which give more than one, two or three periods, the time devoted to community and race relations varies considerably from force to force and with rank. Eight to ten periods at probationer and constable level is a very rough guide to the amount of training given by these forces.

4.7   In our view it is indefensible that some forces give no training in either community or race relations. We believe that all forces should give training in both topics. The resources devoted to each will clearly need to vary according to the features of the force area but we are in no doubt that even forces in rural areas ought to provide some race relations training. We regard this as of particular importance since officers can be promoted, or at times of emergency moved, without warning, into other and different areas. It is in our view quite wrong to expect them to cope with this experience without adequate preparation.

The aims of present training

4.8   If training is to have any impact its aims must be clear. These must inform, and not derive from the content of the course. In their response to our questionnaire forces most often referred to the need to broaden officers' understanding of minority ethnic groups and to the promotion of mutual understanding between the police and the community. Only a few forces said that the aim of their training was to ensure that the attitudes of their officers was correct. In only one case did a force link the aims of training with effective policing. In our view such a link is essential.

Content of present training

4.9   For the most part the content of present training in *community relations* tends to reflect the activities of the force community liaison, or juvenile liaison, department. Liaison with schools is among the most common topics. Others mentioned in the returns we received were: community policing; the community liaison or relations department of the force; the role of the police in society; "attitudes"; "communication"; public relations; and the work of other local statutory agencies. The content of *race relations* training in the great majority of forces consists for the most part of information designed to impart an *understanding* of minority ethnic groups. The topics most commonly covered are: immigration; the cultural and religious backgrounds of the various communities; Government policies as regards race relations and the work of Community Relations Councils and the Commission for Racial Equality. A number of police forces focus on "discrimination" and "prejudice". Another approach is to look at ethnic communities as one of a number of minority groups in respect of which the police may have to take special steps.

4.10 The most serious defect in the content of present training is that for the most part it consists simply of information. Clearly there is some information police officers must have if they are to play an intelligent operational role, but this needs to be local and practical and not, as at present, rather vague and "academic". There is a particular danger in respect of minority ethnic groups that information alone may contribute to stereotyping. In our view, an approach wholly reliant on information is unlikely to prove effective either in promoting real understanding or in affecting attitudes. It is, of course, one consequence of the present preoccupation with information that the need to give officers the practical community and race relations skills they require for the effective discharge of their duties is almost entirely ignored.

Assessment of individual officers

4.11 We note the community and race relations is, alone of all the subjects taken on the initial course at Home Office regional centres and often in later in-force training, unexamined. The requirement to pass an examination or the knowledge that they will be assessed, is, in our view, bound to affect the seriousness with which officers approach the topics in which they receive training and will be taken as a reflection of the importance that the police service attaches to excellence in these areas.

Ranks to whom in-force training is given

4.12 Most forces provide training for probationer constables and sergeants, and the more active also for inspectors. However, while there are some exceptions, very few give any training to higher ranks. A small number of forces indicated that they give training only to selected officers, for example "Home Beat" constables, juvenile liaison or community liaison officers or to those officers serving in divisions where there is a significant minority ethnic population.

4.13 It is, of course, important to remember that in-force training is not the only training that the higher ranks will commonly receive. Community Liaison Officers, for example, are likely to have attended one of the specialist courses hosted by Derbyshire Constabulary and one of the race relations courses held at Holly Royde College, Manchester. In addition the Junior, Intermediate and Senior Command courses at the Police Staff College, Bramshill, contain a substantial element of community and race relations.

4.14 So far as in-force training is concerned we cannot accept that it is right that training should begin to fall away at junior and middle management level as at present, or that virtually no training should be given to the higher ranks. We make clear below (5.3 and 7.1) our belief that regular training should extend to officers of higher ranks both to equip them to discharge their function and responsibilities and, most important, to ensure that the training received by more junior officers is effectively reinforced.

Training methods

4.15 In most forces present training consists of lectures followed by a short discussion. A few adopt a purely 'didactic' approach and dispense with discussion altogether. Some forces use a wider range of methods combining lectures with films, case studies, and visits to local statutory agencies.

Training expertise and materials

4.16 Community and race relations training in most forces is given by the force community liaison (or relations) officer, with contributions from members of minority ethnic communities. The latter are typically drawn from the Commission for Racial Equality, Community Relations Councils, local colleges and universities. Officers from Training Centres or from other police forces are sometimes used. In a handful of police forces representatives of local statutory agencies are brought in to describe the work of their organisations.

4.17 We recognise the operational expertise community liaison officers bring to bear and do not wish to see their experience lost to training. It is, however, clear that if the amount of training given is to be increased and its quality improved in the ways we recommend then fully professional trainers will in future be required. Drawing on our own experience, we believe that it will also be necessary to make greater, and above all much more effective, use of individuals from the minority ethnic communities. We expand on both these points in the final section of our report.

4.18 As regards training materials, we feel that those already in use, though adequate for training as it is presently conducted, will prove neither suitable nor sufficient to support the future training we recommend. For example, the range of films used will have to be more varied and their quality improved. Again, we develop this point in section eight.

The organisation of present training

4.19 To round off this short review of present training we should like to make a number of further points concerned not so much with the content of individual parts of the training or the manner in which they are conducted as with the arrangements for training as a whole. Our first point is that community and race relations training is not at present sufficiently integrated either with training in other topics or with police work generally. The tendency is to treat community and race relations as a separate subject and for instruction in those topics to be given with little thought to how they might most effectively be placed in the training programme. In particular, we feel that far too little care is at present devoted to presenting contributors from minority ethnic communities at the most apt times and in a manner most likely to win them a receptive audience.

4.20 Our second point is that the training given to recruits at the Home Office centres and in-force is not properly co-ordinated. As a result, in-force training now "tops up" regional centre training only in an unguided and unsystematic way. A similar lack of co-ordination affects the training given at different training establishments to higher ranks. We are not, of course, in a position to assess the extent to which the same criticisms may apply to topics other than community and race relations.

THE MAIN PRINCIPLES OF FUTURE TRAINING IN COMMUNITY AND RACE RELATIONS

5.1 In this Section we set down the main principles on which we believe community and race relations training should in future be conducted.

Aims

5.2 The first essential to the success of any training is that it should have clear and realistic aims. As we have already said these aims must inform, and not derive from, the content of courses. The point of all police training must, in our view, be to enhance the effectiveness of the police in all their tasks. Its aims must therefore be as closely related as possible to meeting those needs. Training in community and race relations is no exception. In respect of in-force training the aims set must be related consciously to the community and race relations objectives of each force. The aims of training for each rank are dealt with in detail in Sections 6 and 7.

Extent and Scope

5.3 *All* police officers should receive some community and race relations training and we recommend that training should be given at regular intervals throughout an officer's career up to and including Chief Superintendent. We do not wish to limit the future development of in-force training by specifying in precise terms how much time should be allocated to each topic. But we are clear that the proportion of training courses devoted to them should be substantial and should reflect their central importance to the continued effectiveness of the police. Forces will, of course, need to apportion their resources in the light of the particular problems they face; but for the reasons explained above (paragraph 4.7) all officers should receive some race relations training.

Content

5.4 The content of training should relate closely to the responsibilities of each rank. Courses should include elements designed to increase officers' human and racism awareness; sessions and exercises designed to impart the skills necessary for the proper discharge of the responsibilities of each rank and information about the officers' local community. Training should focus closely on the actual job of practical policing and in particular on those circumstances which can pose difficulties for individual officers or where the force as a whole is less effective in maintaining the support of the community. Especial care needs to be taken over information, especially with regard to minority ethnic groups. Sufficient information must be given to avoid stereotyping and it will be vital to avoid giving the impression that "they" are a population apart from the rest of society and not, as is the fact, an integral part of what is now a multi-racial, multi-cultural society. The guiding principle should be that the information given should be closely related to police work. The content of all courses should be kept up to date and steps should be taken to ensure that it is relevant to current needs.

Training Methods

5.5 We recommend that a full and varied range of methods are used and that care is taken to ensure that the particular methods chosen are well suited to the rank and experience of trainees as well as to the topics being taught. Suitable methods ought, we believe, to include reading, lectures and questions, films, group discussions and structured 'games', case studies, placement with other agencies and role playing. Properly used all these methods can contribute to successful training. (See paragraph 16, Appendix 2.) In particular, we think that role playing, which is already widely used in training for some aspects of police work - for example giving evidence in court - can be invaluable in the teaching of the behavioural and interpersonal skills needed in community and race relations. We note, however, that in race relations in particular, all training undertaken in groups including role playing must be guided by sensitive and experienced trainers who are well acquanted with the pitfalls of such techniques.

Trainers

5.6 We recommend that training should be given by a variety of people. The main burden of training should, we believe, be carried by carefully selected officers with a solid operational record who have professional credibility in the eyes of their colleagues; but that there should

also be a substantial lay involvement. We recommend that individuals fr[...]
communities should be involved both in the design and in the execution of [...]
responsible for training and lay persons (other than those only occasional[...]
themselves receive specialist training. The provision of this specialist trainin[...]
absolutely central to the success of our recommendations. We discuss how it m[...]
and what other measures will be necessary to make the best use of expertise f[...]
police service in Section Eight.

Timing

5.7 We recommend that officers of the rank of sergeant and above should recei[...] training
immediately on promotion and periodically thereafter. In the case of probationers especial care
should be taken to time the various elements of training we recommend in relation to the
officer's growing experience. We attach importance to this principle because community and
race relations training is, we believe, peculiarly liable to be of no effect or counter productive
if it is ill-timed in relation to the acquisition of experience. In particular, information about
minority ethnic groups may simply succeed in leaving young officers with a damagingly
stereotyped view if they have not yet had real personal experience of meeting individuals from
these groups. By the same token training designed to enable officers to deal with difficult
encounters with the public will make little sense until they have had sufficient experience of
these encounters to recognise what may be involved. But if it is important not to give training
too soon it is equally vital not to delay it until bad habits or unacceptable attitudes, which may
be difficult to alter, have formed.

Evaluation of training

5.8 In order that training can be continually improved and keep pace with changing demands
upon it, we recommend that the content, methods, and impact of all training in race and
community relations for all ranks is regularly monitored and assessed. The design of future
training programmes must take account of the need for them to be open to evaluation. A
mixture of criteria will need to be used and it will be important that students' and trainees'
views of courses should be fully taken into account. The real test, however, should be how far
training fulfils its aims, and hence the contribution it makes to the success with which officers
carry out their tasks and the degree to which the goals of the force are met.

5.9 The evaluation of the success of training in community and race relations will not, we
recognise, be an easy task. As a first step we recommend that those involved in training in these
areas take steps to acquaint themselves with the findings of relevant research already underway,
for example the evaluation of Metropolitan Police probationer training being carried out by the
Police Foundation. In the longer term we recommend that resources are made available for such
specific research into suitable evaluative methods as may be necessary.

Assessment of individual officers

5.10 We believe that the assessment of individual police officers both during training and
subsequently is an essential principle of effective training in this field. We make it clear in
Section 6 that, in respect of probationer constables, we favour combining continuous
assessment with a written examination. For these officers in particular, it will be important that
the assessment of performance on courses is not confined to the formal training setting. Any
tendency, for example, to use disrespectful or racial epithets during free time should be noted
and dealt with firmly and expeditiously. So far as officers of higher rank are concerned we note
that they are already assessed as to their attitudes towards, and their ability to communicate
effectively with, all sections of the local community, but we recommend that more formal
arrangements are made to ensure that the full range of community and race relations skills are
assessed. We have given some thought to the form those arrangements should take. The option
we prefer is to invite all Chief Officers to ensure that the report forms used to assess the
performance of their officers should include space specifically for an assessment of officers'
community and race relations performance. We feel that it should be obligatory for this space to
be completed. We envisage that a rounded assessment of police officers would necessitate in the
course of assessment for promotion particular attention being paid to awareness of community
and race relations issues.

first, the training officers receive at each rank and during their subsequent careers must be seen and designed as a whole. The impact that training may have will be lost, and training resources wasted, unless each "block" of training consciously builds on earlier training. Training should be neither haphazard nor repetitive.

5.12 Second, community and race relations training must be well integrated with other subjects dealt with in training programmes. Each part of the community and race relations training must not only be intelligently given in relation to earlier and later training in that subject but should also be well placed in relation to other subjects on the curriculum. The subjects which appear before and after the community and race relations training should be those which illustrate the importance of good community and race relations to particular aspects of police work. Given its importance community and race relations should not be allocated to those sessions on the time-table least conducive to its effectiveness - for example, the final session before a course breaks-up.

5.13 Third, as we imply in paragraph 4.5 above, close attention should be paid to the context in which particular community and race relations skills can best be taught. We have indicated that some time must be set aside for community and race relations topics but the design of training programmes as a whole should take account of the fact that it will often be more effective to teach the necessary skills during training for specific tasks.

FUTURE ARRANGEMENTS FOR COMMUNITY AND RACE RELATIONS TRAINING FOR PROBATIONER CONSTABLES

6.1 Special importance attaches to giving the right training to probationers. It is these officers with whom both during the probationary period and afterwards the public at large will come into most frequent contact. Some, such is the image of the police service presented by the media, will have entered their forces with a narrow conception of the professional roles they will be required to play, and most will be young with little experience of life. In 1979–81 51% of new recruits to the police service in Great Britain (including Scotland) were not yet 21 years old; and about 83% were under 26 years. The importance of good community and race relations, and the need to treat the public of all races in a proper manner must be impressed on recruits right from the very beginning of their careers. Training for these officers must endeavour not merely to give them a full understanding of the jobs they must do and the skill to carry out their tasks in circumstances that may often be difficult; but must consciously attend also to giving them a full and wide experience of dealing with people of all races and from all walks of life.

The aims of training for probationer constables

6.2 We recommend that training in community and race relations for probationer constables should be designed:

   a. to impart a rounded understanding of a police officer's role within a multi-racial society performing many different functions;

   b. to instil an understanding of the need for good community relations and the need to co-operate with other agencies with a role in crime reduction;

   c. to impart a knowledge and sympathetic understanding of the beliefs, customs and attitudes of different groups;

   d. to assist in developing a sense of how discretion can be exercised in a manner best designed to secure effective policing and ensure good relations with the public;

   e. to encourage officers to carry our their duties in a manner which does not alienate the public and to equip them with the social skills necessary for the effective policing of a multi-cultural community, especially under stress and in situations which typically cause difficulty;

   f. to give individual officers an understanding of the need for good race relations and an insight into their own attitudes and prejudices; and insofar as these attitudes and prejudices are inimical to effective policing to modify them for the better.

Outline of probationary training

6.3 We understand that the Working Party on Probationer Training is likely to endorse the view that the whole of the two year probationary period should be regarded as an apprenticeship during which the recruit's policing skills are progressively developed under supervision. We commend this approach. In outline, the course of instruction in community and race relations which we recommend below is designed to mix periods of formal training to be undertaken in central or force training establishments with training on the job in a manner which will capitalise on the strengths of each. The content of the course is calculated initially to introduce recruits to the demands on them; the central importance of good community and race relations to the effectiveness of the police; and thereafter to ensure that their attitudes to the public of all races are correct and to equip them with the necessary information and skills.

Community and race relations training for probationer constables.

Initial training at training centres

6.4 We envisage that the first 'block' of community and race relations training will be given in future, as it is now, at Home Office regional training centres. The Working Party on probationer training will suggest what length the initial course should be. For our part we note only that we do not wish to see the bulk of the community and race relations training that probationer constables will receive confined to this initial course, even if it is extended in length. We believe that the *initial* community and race relations course should do no more than provide a firm base for future training and on the job experience. At Appendix 3 we list the topics which we believe should be covered. We recommend that the objective of this part of the training should be to equip students with the minimum knowledge and understanding which they will need to function *under supervision* when they return to their forces; to provide a sound foundation on which later training can progressively be built; and to set the high standards of personal behaviour required.

Initial training within individual police forces

6.5 We do not believe that this short course alone can adequately prepared probationer constables to go out on the streets unsupervised. We would hope that on return to their forces recruits will be given intensive instruction in "streetcraft" by way of a special 'street duties' course and a period under the supervision of an experienced "tutor" constable. The purpose of this training will, of course, be to give probationer constables their first taste of the full range and pressures of police work. We would hope that the opportunity will be taken to illustrate the importance of community and race relations for practical, everyday policing. In particular we believe that this period of training will provide a timely opportunity to impart some of the information that it is necessary for police officers to have. This information should include an introduction to some of the premises and locations in the community which may be important to sensitive and effective policing and the individuals locally whom it may be disirable for officers to know including those working in other local agencies and services.

6.6 Following their introduction to practical policing we would envisage that the primary purpose of in-force training for probationers should be to develop their street experience. During this period probationer constables should be given an insight into the way policing is geared to local needs and problems. We have carefully considered Lord Scarman's recommendation (paragraph 5.26 of his report) that an officer's period on probation should include, if possible, a period in a city area where "ethnic minorities form a substantial proportion of the population". We well understand the reasons for this recommendation. On balance, however we have concluded that the practical difficulties will be insurmountable; and that in any event officers for whom this experience would be appropriate would be unlikely to gain sufficient insight into the complexities of policing these areas in the time that could be made available. In our view, the only practicable and effective way of preparing young officers from rural forces to undertaking any special duties they may from time to time be called on to perform in city areas is by ensuring that these officers receive adequate public order training which takes full account of the particular sensitivity of community and race relations in these areas.

Subsequent training for probationer constables

6.7 At about six months into the probationary period we recommend that probationers should be given a short course on community and race relations either at a Home Office regional centre or at a force training establishment. The precise timing will need to take account of the arrangements recommended by the Working Party on Probationer Training but it will we believe be important for the course to take place after probationers have gained some real experience of police work but *before* any unacceptable attitudes have taken hold. Performance on this course must be fully assessed.

6.8 The course we envisage should aim to build on the initial course at the Home Office regional training centres and the pattern of training experience we have recommended and should include the following three elements:

    a. study of the topics treated in the initial course in greater depth and with greater student participation;

    b. training in the specific inter-personal and behavioural (including non-verbal) skills needed to deal confidently and sensitively with the public; and

    c. racism awareness training.

6.9   The aim of the first element would be to remind students of what they were taught on the initial course and to allow them to explore the concepts involved and the issues raised in greater depth and to relate them to their practical experience to date.

6.10 We suggest that b., skills training, should also be designed to give officers an insight into their own behaviour and into how they appear to others. It will be particularly important that the following features are incorporated:

  i.   emphasis on *practical* skills needed in "nuts and bolts" situations;

  ii.   extensive use of role playing as a training method; and

  iii. assessment by a variety of methods, including self-assessment and student feedback.

6.11 Students will clearly gain many of the skills and much of the insight and self-knowledge required in their dealings with individuals of a different race from the training described in paragraph 6.10 above. However, in recognition of the special difficulties which exist we recommend that a distinct but *allied* course of training in racism awareness is also given to probationers at this stage in their careers. Such a course, which must be guided by expert "facilitators", should encourage recruits to uncover, understand and deal with any prejudices they might have; to understand the roots of any hostility shown to them as representatives of a predominantly white authority; and to cope with the subtleties of any culturally conditioned reactions they may meet. The sort of training we have in mind here was developed by Ms Judith Katz in America and has been adapted for use in this country by the Racism Awareness Unit. The training offered by this Unit is briefly described in Appendix 4.

6.12 We suggest this course should be followed by further on the job experience interspersed with formal training *related to identified community and race relations problems faced by the probationer's force.* The emphasis of this formal training should be on the progress made by individual officers. During this period probationers will need close and continual supervision. In Section 8 we made a number of suggestions as to how supervisors might be helped in their task. The success of in-force training should be measured.

Final period in a training establishment

6.13 To round off the probationary period it is suggested that recruits return to a training establishment. This will give an opportunity for students to review the training they have received and for any faults that remain to be corrected. Students should be required to exhibit in written work, in training exercises and in their conduct at the establishment that they have a thorough grasp of what is required by way of skills and attitudes conducive to good community and race relations. Arrangements should be made for an overall assessment to be available to their own force. We recommend that it should be obligatory to take this final assessment into account in deciding whether or not a probationer's appointment is to be confirmed.

COMMUNITY AND RACE RELATIONS TRAINING FOR CONSTABLES (OTHER THAN PROBATIONERS), SERGEANTS, INSPECTORS AND HIGHER RANKS.

7.1 The special importance which attaches to giving appropriate training to probationers should not overshadow the vital necessity of giving training to constables and more senior ranks. We believe that the functions and responsibilities of each rank call for a distinctive training programme. In particular officers at junior and middle management level need to be equipped to understand the importance of supervising more junior officers in a manner that reinforces the training they will have received. It would not, we believe, be appropriate to recommend training *in terms* for the most senior management level but these officers must play an important part in ensuring that training is effective. They have a particular responsibility for ensuring that the ethos of the force is right, that good performance in race and community relations is adequately rewarded, and that supervising officers of lower rank are discharging their duties in a satisfactory manner. Above all, they must ensure that the right policies as regards race and community relations are adopted and practiced throughout the force and that in-force training is well designed to carry these policies forward. If there is to be a point in an officer's career where *formal* and *regular* training is to be regarded as no longer appropriate than it should be at the level where officers cease to be responsible for the detail of day to day operations in a particular division or locality and take on board management responsibilities for the force as a whole.

7.2 We should begin by making one general point. We have commented at some length on the inadequacies of present training in race and community relations. Indeed many officers in post will have received virtually no training at all. If training is to contribute substantially to improvements in relations between the police and the community, and, more importantly, the present generation of supervisory officers are to reinforce the training received by their juniors in the way we recommend, then an effort must be made to enable them to "catch up" on the training we recommend for the future. We think it of particular importance that *all* officers should receive race relations, especially racism awareness, training. We recognise that even if our recommendations with regard to the future provision of specialist trainers are accepted, resources will remain limited and logistical problems may arise. For this reason we recommend that priority should be given to more senior officers.

Constables

7.3 Following any necessary "catching up" courses we recommend that constables are given short "refresher" courses, within individual police forces, with the following aims:

a. to remind them of the importance of the lessons imparted by their probationer (or "catching up") training;

b. to draw on their increasing experience to broaden and deepen their understanding of their role in the community;

c. to sharpen their community and race relations skills and their racism awareness;

d. to counter any tendency to cynicism, personal rigidity, or inflexibility in dealing with the public;

e. to counter any tendency to racial stereotyping;

f. draw on their increasing experience to support new ways in which they can put their community and race relations training into practice.

7.4 The emphasis of these courses should increasingly be on the participation of constables as they gain in experience. For those with substantial service, courses might consist largely of group discussions and be aimed as much at encouraging officers to reflect critically on their experience as at the formal transmission of ideas or practices. The sessions can be informal but they should be regular.

Training for functional specialists

7.5 *In addition* to the above training, we recommend that opportunities should be taken to inject a substantial community and race relations element into any training for specialist work such as CID or traffic duties undertaken by constables. Much specialist training will continue, of course, to be devoted to ensuring that officers are technically proficient; but a high priority should nevertheless be placed on ensuring that specialist duties are carried out with proper regard to the dignity of individuals and to their effect on community and race relations. The aim should be to ensure that officers fully understand that their behaviour in dealing with, and attitudes towards, members of the public will be an important determinant of their effectiveness. To encourage proper attitudes and standards, officers' performance in community and race relations as well as their technical competence should be assessed and count towards whether or not they are accepted as full-time specialists. This will be particularly important where employment in a specialty is regarded as status enhancing.

"Home Beat" Officers and "Tutor Constables"

7.6 We believe that "home beat" officers or "community" officers ought to receive special training beyond that given to other police constables. Such officers must display a particularly keen appreciation of the subtleties of policing and of the need to involve the local community in the reduction of crime and a real feel for race relations. There are, in addition, a number of respects in which their need for an understanding of how the community and other agencies besides the police service function is greater than that of other constables. For example, officers working with local tenants groups, as many home beat officers do increasingly, require not only a basic understanding of the workings of local democracy but a detailed knowledge of the everyday working practices of other agencies. Similarly, constables policing housing estates require an intimate practical knowledge of how the various local authority agencies function if they are to serve the community effectively.

7.7 We accept that much of the expertise of home beat officers can be gained only by experience. We believe nonetheless that training can contribute to the effectiveness of this vital area of police work. All constables should, of course, ideally possess the knowledge required by a good home beat officer and be fully alive to the effect that their conduct may have on community and race relations; and we would stress that by suggesting that these officers require additional training we do not mean to imply that responsibility for achieving a close relationship with the community should rest exclusively on their shoulders. In practical terms, however, we are clear that additional training for those officers is desirable. We also feel that a recognition of the *additional* training needs of home beat officers could also help to raise their status within the police service; and that assessment of their performance in training within individual forces should also provide senior management with valuable assistance in selecting the right officers for this sensitive work.

7.8 We recognise that as a general rule forces already give some special preparation to their tutor constables and that officers selected for this role are experienced and mature. But we recommend that those selected to be tutor constables should be given adequate training in the supervisory skills necessary to ensure that constables in their charge put into practice the community and race relations lessons of their earlier training, and that basic faults in attitude or behaviour are corrected.

7.9 As we have made clear, we feel that there is a need to inject an element of community and race relations instruction into training for specialists. Close attention must also be paid to training for any special duties that constables may be required to undertake from time to time. It is important that such duties are not regarded as in any way separate from the mainstream of police work and hence without the same implications for community and race relations. The reverse may often be the case. We recommend, accordingly, that those responsible for public order training, training for the policing of demonstrations and public events, and for participation in police support or other special units, should endeavour to draw out the aspects of these duties that are of particular importance for good community and race relations.

Training for police officers from Sergeants to Chief Superintendents

7.10 In each of these ranks, we believe that police officers should receive some training which is both formal and regular. Whilst there will clearly be significant differences between ranks in the content and methods used and in the depth in which topics are studied, we recommend that training for all supervisors of junior and middle management should, building on the basic aims in paragraphs 5.2 and 6.2, share the following broad objectives:

   a. to ensure that officers' personal behaviour and attitudes' as regards community and race relations are in accordance with the highest professional standards;

   b. to impart an understanding appropriate to the officer's rank of a modern pluralist multi-racial society; and of the ethical and operational importance of good community and race relations, with all that that implies;

   c. to ensure that officers at each level are aware of their responsibility for the proper supervision of their subordinates and of the need for training in race and community relations to be reinforced;

   d. to equip officers at each level with the appropriate qualities of leadership and the necessary management and supervisory skills to enable them effectively to ensure that officers under their command achieve and maintain acceptable standards in community and race relations; and

   e. to help officers with the task of assessing more junior police officers.

7.11 In the light of our recommendations in Section 5 we suggest that the following principles should inform training for all junior and middle management ranks. In particular training at each rank should:

   i. build on that given earlier in the officer's career;

   ii. relate to the actual functions and responsibilities of the job at that level;

   iii. where possible be thoroughly integrated with other topics on the courses;

   iv. in line with (iii) above be given whenever training in any other topic or speciality is undertaken;

   v. be given first immediately on the officers' assumption of his new responsibilities, and thereafter at regular intervals;

   vi. be fully assessed.

Contacts with the community

7.12 Throughout their careers officers should be encouraged to develop sustained and positive contacts with their local community. To help forge such contacts individual officers of all ranks, but particularly more senior officers might, where practicable, be given the opportunity from time to time to spend short periods in placements designed to acquaint them with the work of other agencies whose responsibilities overlap or contrast with those of the police, and to mix with members of the community in a social or work setting. Such opportunities might in part be provided during time set aside for training. Care should be taken to tailor such occasional placements to the needs of the individual officer; and in the case of younger officers to ensure that their experience is properly structured and guided by their supervisors.

7.13 With the objectives and principles described in paragraphs 7.10 and 7.11 above in mind we suggest below some of the more important topics that might be covered at each stage of an officer's career, and some of the more important considerations that apply to training at each rank. We make no attempt to spell out comprehensively the content of the required training. Instead we concentrate on the *additional* training that officers in a particular rank may need over the training that they will have received at a lower rank. This reflects our belief that effective training must be related to the specific jobs done by officers at each rank.

Sergeants

7.14 We recommend that where necessary sergeants should receive the "catching up" courses envisaged at 7.2. Special emphasis should be given to:

   i. the scope for, and techniques of, local accountability;

   ii. the need to involve the community in long and short term measures designed to reduce crime;

   iii. co-operation with other agencies;

   iv. policing "styles" ("reactive" and "proactive" etc);

   v. the exercise of discretion;

   vi. the need to support the victims of crime;

   vii. basic psychology of the individual.

The purpose of (iv) above should be to encourage officers to be flexible and open minded in their thinking, to see the police service as the community may see it, and above all to consider carefully the level and style of response which may be required in different situations involving persons of different cultural backgrounds. Such training should involve the extensive use of case studies — preferably real examples — of problems requiring flexible thinking and a delicate touch. At this level officers might also explore in some depth the functions and responsibilities of other agencies which may also have a role to play in dealing with these and other problems.

7.15 Training should leave officers in no doubt that it is their responsibility to ensure that officers under their supervision put the training they receive into practice. To fulfill this part of their function officers will need fully to appreciate their role in reinforcing the lessons of training.

7.16 For the most part the management and supervisory skills required to ensure that the community and race relations aspects of police work are satisfactorily discharged by subordinates will not differ from those required in the exercise of the general range of management responsibilities of the rank. We feel however, that special training will be required in three areas:

   i. the assessment of performance in race and community relations, especially though not exclusively, as regards probationers;

   ii. the techniques of dealing with racist behaviour (verbal and non-verbal) in a manner which is not counter productive;

   iii. the identification and reversal of any tendency towards cynicism on the part of more junior officers.

Inspectors and Chief Inspectors

7.17 We recommend that police officers in these ranks should also receive "catching up" training.

7.18 We believe that these officers should explore in more depth than they will have done in earlier training the concept of institutional racism. To develop their understanding of how any institutional racism in the police service can be identified and tackled they will require training in addition to that designed to overcome personal discrimination.

7.19 That apart, the main additional requirement for these ranks is for training designed to encourage officers to begin to see their work in a wider context and to give them a rounded understanding of the role (and legitimacy) of elected and other representatives (including pressure groups). "General Studies" topics to be given special attention should include some basic criminology (including further and deeper study of the criminal justice system); and the techniques of, and different approaches possible, to the reduction of crime. On the operational side, emphasis should be placed on:

    (i)   consultation with the community and the ways in which the community's policing needs can be assessed and competing claims balanced;

    (ii) the balance to be struck between enforcing the law and keeping the peace;

    (iii) study of the relative advantages and impact of different policing styles and their implications for race and community relations.

7.20 Police officers at these ranks will require training in management and supervisory techniques which reinforces that recommended for sergeants.

Superintendents and Chief Superintendents

7.21 We recommend that officers at these ranks should also receive "catching up" training. We believe that these officers also need a deeper understanding than their subordinates of the nature and ramifications of institutional discrimination and of the steps which might be taken to eradicate it.

7.22 At this level officers will need a thorough and sympathetic knowledge of the political context in which they work. Special topics should include:

    (i)   democracy at the local and national level;

    (ii) cultural relativism and equality before the law;

    (iii) studies of other enforcement agencies, or problems of a legal or quasi-legal nature dealt with by other agencies;

    (iv) the basic sociology of different social and racial groups.

Besides such topics, which should be taught in a practical job-related and not purely academic fashion, training at this level should allow the opportunity for officers to explore new and different ways in which familiar operational problems, past solutions to which may have elicited an adverse response, might in future be resolved. Such training might use case studies based on real incidents that have recently occurred and might in effect constitute a step by step critical reappraisal of past action.

7.23 In addition to training designed to impress on officers their role in reinforcing the lessons of training officers at these ranks should also have an understanding of the critical importance of their setting the correct "tone".

7.24 The special additional need for these ranks is for training in the supervision of large scale, or otherwise sensitive, operations which unless well handled may alienate the community from the police. The management and supervisory skills needed at these ranks will not otherwise differ essentially from those required at lower ranks, the main skills required being: to know first of all who to assign to what duties; to appreciate when *personal* involvement is needed to ensure that operations are professionally conducted; and to ensure that subordinates never lose sight of the implications of their actions for race and community relations. Management skill will also be required to ensure that in so far as the operational and community relations sides of the force are functionally distinct they pull together and consult as necessary.

Training methods for police officers from Sergeants to Chief Superintendents

7.25 We recommend that training for sergeants should broadly use the same full range of methods adopted for constables, but with greater emphasis on student participation and the preparation of individual projects. For example, reading, discussions, and presentations should form a substantial part of the community and race relations content of courses. Thereafter training for more senior ranks should progressively seek to develop the officer's individual initiative and elicit from him such personal contributions as may benefit the training of the group and hence the service as a whole. From time to time sergeants and inspectors might be asked to demonstrate their understanding of race and community relations by project work perhaps followed by a presentation. Examples of the topics which might be covered in this way are: how a particular style of policing locally has fared in practice; and the fruits of collaboration with other agencies in contact with individuals. Outside speakers, including minority ethnic contributors should be fully involved in training for all ranks.

Assistant Chief Constables and above

7.26 We recommend that as an essential and integral part of the training process officers at the highest level should periodically come together for seminars or discussions, the purpose of which should be to examine the community and race relations performance of their forces with a view to identifying any strengths and deficiencies and suggesting how training could help to improve performance in the future. In brief, such seminars or discussions should seek to ensure that:

(i)   force policies and hence training are appropriate to the problems faced by forces; and keep pace with changing circumstances;

(ii) training (wherever undertaken) is consistent with and well designed to take forward force policies with regard to race and community relations;

(iii) officers are being full and accurately assessed as to their community and race relations performance and that good performance is being properly recognised;

(iv) the "ethos" of forces is conducive to good community and race relations and that the most senior officers are setting a clear and explicit example to all ranks (including the most junior) and doing their personal best to ensure that the correct attitudes are conveyed to lower ranks; and, most important,

(v)   management practices are well designed to ensure that practices and attitudes commended by the most senior officers are adopted throughout the force and that there are clear and effective channels for obtaining "feedback" from ranks down to constables as to the effectiveness of force community and race relations policies at street level.

We envisage that, while in large forces, for example, the Metropolitan Police, senior officers might usefully attend such gatherings within their own force, elsewhere senior officers from a number of forces could join together for these seminars.

TRAINING EXPERTISE AND MATERIALS

8.1 It is clear to us that the police service does not make either sufficient or the best possible use of the expertise available at present outside the police service. This is particularly true of minority ethnic contributors. In force areas with significant minority ethnic communities we recommend that many more contributors from these communities than at present should be invited to take part in the training of officers of all ranks. Because of their experience and background people from minority ethnic communities have an indispensible contribution to make, in particular to race relations training. We think it of the highest importance, however, that the experience of training does not itself contribute to stereotyping. For this reason, we recommend that wherever possible individuals from minority ethnic communities are invited along with other lay people and police officers to give training in subjects other than race. In time we would, of course, hope to see serving officers from minority ethnic communities playing their part but the temptation to use such officers simply as a training resource must be strenuously resisted. We should make it clear that we also wish to see a greater contribution not simply from individuals from minority ethnic groups but from suitably experienced lay people generally.

8.2 If there is a need to increase lay involvement then there also is a need to ensure that their contributions are integrated with the rest of the course in such a way as to have maximum impact and are more closely tailored than at present to the specific requirements of the police service. To this end we recommend that the help of lay people, including those from minority ethnic communities, is enlisted on a more active and permanent basis than hitherto. In particular they must be invited to contribute to the design of, and not merely the execution of, training programmes. We recognise that there will, of course, remain a need for less regular contributors. In these cases such contributors must be fully briefed as to what is required from them and the context in which the training they offer will take place.

8.3 Improvements in the use of the expertise available at present will be valuable but if the training we recommend is to be successful much more radical measures will need to be taken. There will, in particular be a pressing need to provide a sufficient number of instructors who can bring — particularly to race relations training — the skill, sensitivity and imagination demanded. Experience in the United States suggests that to give them the necessary level of expertise instructors will need *specialist training courses of at least sixteen weeks.* One special need will be for an adequate number of "facilitators" to give the racism awareness training we recommend. These facilitators will require a more certain "feel" for race relations and a higher level of training expertise. The need for suitable training materials will also be urgent. Some of the existing — largely American — material (literature and films) will remain useful and should not be discarded lightly but there is simply not enough material available at present and what there is cannot be adopted wholesale. We discuss below how we believe these needs should be met.

8.4 One immediate problem will be to provide a first batch of instructors and facilitators. We recommend that as a first step a small number of carefully selected officers and lay individuals who will be involved in police training should be sent to one or more specialist establishments or units, in this country or overseas, such as the United States Department of Defense Equal Opportunity Management Institute (EOMI) at Patrick Air Force Base, Florida, to receive the race relations training given there. So far as the latter institute is concerned we acknowledge that while race relations training for the American Military aims to resolve problems arising within the various armed services, training for police officers in this country will need to be designed to help improve the relationship between the police service and the public. The training provided elsewhere may also be specifically designed to respond to problems faced by services other than the police. We nevertheless believe that the experience of the training these establishments can offer would provide a core of future instructors with sufficient insights into how race relations training should be given to enable them to help design a special course suitable for the training of a first full generation of trainers for the police service.

8.5 Equally pressing is the need to introduce racism awareness training. We recommend that such training is introduced without delay initially in a number — perhaps two — of neighbouring force areas and that a pilot study is made of its impact. We know that the Racism Awareness

Programme Unit (RAPU) is ready to help the service train police officers as "facilitators" for this type of training and we recommend that police forces look to them, and to other organisations in the field, for expert guidance. Subject to a favourable evaluation of the pilot study, we hope that thereafter racism awareness training will be given to all police officers as soon as practicable.

8.6 Our recommendations above will not by themselves meet the continuing need to provide expert trainers and facilitators. We cannot give a precise estimate but it is clear that they will be required in considerable numbers. Large forces will require an adequate and permanent complement of specialist instructors. To make the best use of resources and to ensure that expertise, particularly in race relations, is available to forces which may have fewer officers to train, we recommend that a number of specialist instructors should be employed in a "roving" capacity. By this we mean that these instructors should not be confined to one particular force or training establishment but should circulate so as to provide a training resource upon which a number of forces could draw. Their primary purpose would be to assist in giving in-force training and to provide an expert resource on which supervisors could draw.

8.7 We have made clear our conviction that in future community and race relations training must make use of a wide variety of methods. The need for new training materials is therefore considerable. These materials will need to include lecture notes, case studies, role playing scenarios, some structured group "games", literature on current issues and good films. This material, particularly where it is used to teach the skills involved in dealing with difficult encounters with members of the public, will need careful and expert development. If role playing scenarios are to be of real help to individual officers they will need to be based on detailed and objective observational studies of actual events. The nature of these encounters and the skills required to deal successfully with them need to be analysed and documented. As Appendix 2 (paragraph 17) makes clear while some work analysing the detail of police encounters with the public has been done in the United States no comparable research has been undertaken in this country. We believe that such research will be essential to underpin future skills training and we recommend that it is carried out without delay.

8.8 It will take time to develop these materials but progress can, we believe, be made quickly. In particular we believe that television can provide many useful and topical illustrations of the sort of difficulties police officers can encounter and which may have implications for their relationship with the public: and we therefore recommend that arrangements are made with television companies to secure the release and use of excerpts of television programmes and news bulletins for training purposes. In the longer term, however, as we have made clear, special materials will be needed. For example, so far as films are concerned, what will be needed is material geared to the British experience. We would stress that, as with other materials, these films must be of good quality and should not suffer in comparison with the standard of British television programmes. They might, as have some recent and highly successful management training films, employ well known actors and actresses. The best use must, of course, be made of resources but material which is obviously amateurish will, we believe, do little good and probably some harm.

8.9 At the same time any existing materials, including those designed to support training in topics other than community and race relations, especially if they appear otherwise suitable for future use, should be carefully scrutinised to ensure that they are also well designed to encourage a sensitive approach to community relations.

The longer term

8.10 These immediate steps are necessary but will not be sufficient. We are clear that in the longer term the need for specialist training and materials can only be met by the establishment of a new training support centre. This centre should have the following functions:

(i)   To provide specialist courses for serving police officers and others regularly responsible for community and race relations training.

(ii) To assist police forces in the effective use of occasional contributors, including individuals from minority ethnic communities, and to provide those contributors with help and advice.

(iii) To develop and disseminate a full range of specialist training materials.

(iv) To inform forces of the findings of research relevant to training, including work on evaluative methods suitable for use in this field and on the assessment of individual performance.

8.11 A new centre catering only for the needs of the police service might, of course, be held to suggest that the police are uniquely in need of race relations training. This is clearly far from the case and we are of the view that it is in principle highly desirable that it should aim eventually to provide a resource for more than one profession with an acknowledged need for training of this kind. A multi profession centre would provide the setting for an exchange of professional perspectives on common problems and inform and enhance the training given to each group. We feel, too, that if a number of services can share this common facility then inter-agency co-operation between them at a local level will be encouraged.

8.12 We cannot give a precise estimate of the resources that will be required to establish the new centre but we do not believe that the cost should, in total, be prohibitive and we hope that every priority will be given to providing the necessary funds. As to manpower, we have in mind only a small working team who would act as a catalyst to bring about a rapid and effective development of the training required. We acknowledge, too, that there are many practical questions, for example, over location, that will need to be answered before the centre can be established. We hope that these will be tackled without delay. For our part we would see some merit in attaching the centre to an independent institution (eg a university) particularly, if in time, it is to serve several professions; though we recognise that if delay is to be avoided then it may initially have to serve only the police service and to be based within it.

Future action

8.13 As we have made clear, it will fall to the separate Working Party examining the training given to probationer constables and to those responsible for reviewing training in the handling of public disorder, and supervision and management training, to decide how best to incorporate our recommendations on community and race relations training into the wider training programmes which they envisage. We accept that the full introduction of the training we have recommended will therefore take some time. There should, however, be no unnecessary delay. On the assumption that our report will prove acceptable, we think that there would be advantage in making our proposals known to those in Home Office and force training establishments who will have the task of implementing them. Some of our ideas could well be tried out within the existing system. On other immediate action, we suggest that:

a. research should be put in hand on encounters between the police and public (8.7);

b. a pilot study of racism awareness training should be mounted in one or two forces (8.5);

c. a small number of carefully selected officers should receive the training available at EOMI or elsewhere (8.4);

d. work preliminary to the establishment of a new training and resources centre should be undertaken.

SUMMARY OF CONCLUSIONS

9.1   A summary of our main conclusions follows.

GENERAL CONCLUSIONS

Present in-force training

(i)   There are a number of serious weaknesses in present "in-force" training. Not all forces give training in community and race relations and few give training to ranks above sergeant. The aims of such training as is given are generally unclear and unrelated to the practical requirements of the police service. The most serious defect in the content of present training is that it consists, for the most part, simply of information. A narrow range of methods is used and neither the training nor individual officers are assessed. Training is not organised to maximum effect. Expertise and materials available, while adequate for present training, will not be so in future (paragraphs 4.6 - 4.20).

Main principles of future training

Scope

(ii)   *All* officers should in future receive training in community and race relations (paragraph 5.3)

(iii)   In particular, although forces should apportion their resources in the light of the particular problems they face, all officers should receive *adequate race relations* training (paragraphs 4.7 and 5.3).

(iv)   Where they have not in the past received adequate training officers must be enabled to "catch up" on the training, particularly the racism awareness training, recommended for the future (paragraph 7.2).

(v)   Regular training should be given at intervals throughout an officer's career up to and including the rank of chief superintendent. The most senior ranks have a vital role to play (paragraphs 5.3, and 7.1).

Features

(vi)   There are good reasons for teaching community and race relations together but the relationship between the police and the public is more complex where race is an issue and some time should consciously be set aside for instruction focussed specifically on race relations (paragraph 2.4).

(vii)   Strategically, training should be aimed at both attitudes and behaviour. Attitude training must go hand in hand with the teaching of effective policing skills (paragraph 2.6).

(viii) Training must aim to enhance the effectiveness with which the police carry out all their duties. It must therefore be as closely related as possible to the requirements of individual officers and to the community and race relations objective of each force (paragraph 5.2).

(ix)   Training for probationer constables should be carefully timed in relation to the acquisition of experience; that for other ranks should be given immediately on promotion and periodically thereafter (paragraph 5.7).

(x)   The content of training should focus on the day to day job of policing and should include: information of practical use about the officer's local community; human and racism awareness training; and instruction in the behavioural skills necessary to deal with encounters with the public, especially those which may cause difficulty (paragraph 5.4).

(xi)   A distinctive programme of training should be given to officers at each rank, the content of which should relate closely to their responsibilities (paragraphs 5.4 and 7.1).

(xii) A full and varied range of training methods should be used. In particular role playing should be used in the teaching of behavioural skills (paragraph 5.5).

(xiii) The main burden of training should be carried by officers with a solid operational record who have professional credibility in the eyes of their colleagues. But there should also be a substantial lay involvement including individuals from minority ethnic communities (paragraph 5.6).

(xiv) Community and race relations training must be well integrated with, and carefully placed among, other subjects in the curriculum. Trainers in all subjects should draw out the lessons for community and race relations (paragraphs 4.5, 5. 12 and 5.13).

(xv) Community and race relations training should in future be evaluated. Resources should be made available for such specific research into suitable evaluative methods as may be necessary (paragraph 5.9).

(xvi) An essential ingredient of effective training should be an appropriate method of assessing individual officers in relation to community and race relations both during formal training and subsequently. For probationer constables we favour combining continuous assessment with a written examination. Assessment for promotion should pay particular attention to the officer's sensitivity to community and race relations issues (paragraph 5.10).

OUTLINE OF CONCLUSIONS ON FUTURE TRAINING ARRANGEMENTS

Probationer constables

(i) Community and race relations training should be designed to mix periods of formal training to be undertaken in central or force training establishments with training on the job in a manner which will capitalise on the strengths of each (paragraph 6.3).

(ii) The initial course at Home Office regional training centres should concentrate on providing a firm base for future training and on the job experience; and on equipping probationers with the minimum knowledge and understanding which they will need to function under supervision when they return to their forces (paragraph 6.4).

(iii) On return to their forces recruits should be given intensive instruction in "streetcraft", including information about their local community (paragraph 6.5).

(iv) After probationers have gained some real experience of police work but before any unacceptable attitudes have taken hold, they should undertake a further course at a training establishment. The course should include training in interpersonal and behavioural skills and in racism awareness (paragraphs 6.7 — 6.11 and appendix 4).

(v) Probationers should receive further on the job experience and formal in-force training related to identified community and race relations problems faced by their force before returning for a final period of instruction at a training establishment. Arrangements should be made for individual probationers to be assessed in relation to community and race relations. It should be obligatory for forces to take this assessment into account in deciding whether or not a probationer's appointment is to be confirmed (paragraph 6.12 and 6.13).

Police Constables

(vi) Constables should periodically receive short "refresher" courses with the aims set out in paragraph 7.3.

(vii) Community and race relations training should be given to functional specialists and in relation to special duties (paragraphs 7.5 — 7.9).

Sergeants to Chief Superintendents

(viii) Officers at junior and middle management level should be equipped to understand the importance of supervising more junior officers in a manner that reinforces the training they will have received (paragraph 7.1). The training required by sergeants is described in paragraphs 7.14 – 7.16. Among the topics which should be given to officers at this rank is policing "styles", the purpose of which will be to demonstrate with reference to real examples the practical problems that require flexible thinking and a delicate touch (paragraph 7.14).

Inspectors and Chief Inspectors

(ix) The main *additional* requirements for officers at these ranks is for training designed to encourage them to begin to see their work in a wider context and to impart an understanding of institutional racism (paragraphs 7.18 and 7.19).

Superintendents and Chief Superintendents

(x) Officers at this level need a thorough and sympathetic knowledge of the political context in which they work and in the supervision of large scale, or otherwise sensitive, operations (paragraphs 7.22 and 7.24).

Senior Management

(xi) Officers of ranks above chief superintendent should hold seminars and discussions on the lines described in paragraph 7.26.

CONCLUSIONS ON THE PROVISION OF EXPERT TRAINERS AND MATERIALS

(i) Better use should be made of the expertise and teaching materials available at present. Lay people, including individuals from minority ethnic communities should be involved on a large scale and in both the design and execution of ʼng programmes (paragraphs 8.1 and 8.2).

(ii) More radical steps, however, will have ʼpecialist trainers and new materials required (paragraph 8.3

(iii) A new specialist and intensive cour ʼed. One immediate step towards its development shoul umber of carefully selected officers and lay people to ʼStates Department of Defence Equal Opportunities Mar ʼorce Base, Florida (paragraph 8.4).

(iv) At the same time, racism awarenes hout delay and a pilot study be made of its impact (

(v) To assist the development of the ʼing in practical policing skills, detailed, observat ʼto difficult encounters between the police and t

(vi) In the longer term the need for be met by the establishment of a new training provide specialist courses for trainers, new materi eventual aim might be that the centre should provide a re of professions (paragraphs 8.10 and 8.11).

IMMEDIATE ACTION

There should be no unnecessary delay in introducing the new training recommended in this report. Immediate action should be taken on (iii), (iv) and (v) above and on the preliminary groundwork necessary to the establishment of the new centre (vi). Our proposals might be made known immediately to officers concerned with the development of training (paragraph 8.13).

POLICE TRAINING COUNCIL
WORKING PARTY ON COMMUNITY AND RACE RELATIONS TRAINING FOR THE POLICE

MEMBERS

Mr J L Bantock (Chairman)	Home Office Police Department
Mr R W Adcock	Association of County Councils
Dr M Argyle and subsequently Dr J Shapland	Academic Adviser
Mr P Boateng	Association of Metropolitan Authorities
Sir James Crane CBE	HM Chief Inspector of Constabulary
Mr B A Emes	Home Office Police Department
Mr T R Hall	Rugby Community Relations Council
Dr F S Hashmi, CBE	Commission for Racial Equality
Chief Superintendent N Hird and subsequently Chief Superintendent T J W Hill	Police Superintendents Association
Deputy Assistant Commissioner R Hunt, subsequently Deputy Assistant Commissioner C Smith, then Deputy Assistant Commissioner J Radley, QPM	Metropolitan Police
Inspector E P Johnson	Police Federation
Sir Philip Knights, CBE, QPM	Training Committee, Association of Chief Police Officers of England and Wales
Ms D Kuya	Race Relations and Ethnic Adviser for the London Borough of Haringey
Miss N Peppard, CBE	Home Office Race Relations Adviser

Secretariat

Mr A F C Crook	Home Office Police Department
Mr K D Sutton	Home Office Police Department

The following also attended on one or more occasions

Chief Superintendent D Badham	For Sir James Crane
Mr R H Barton, QPM	For Sir James Crane
Mr R F Broome	For Sir Philip Knights
Mr W Bryant	Home Office Police Department
Chief Superintendent R Coulson	Police Superintendents Association
Sergeant A Crow	Police Federation
Mr C Griffiths	For Mr Boateng
Chief Superintendent A Halford	Metropolitan Police
Captain M J Marriott	Director of Human Resources Management Program, US Navy Europe
Chief Inspector I McKenzie	Metropolitan Police
Mr N L Morgan	Home Office Police Department
Commander R B Wells	Metropolitan Police

POLICE TRAINING IN RACE RELATIONS: SOME RESEARCH EVIDENCE

This paper reviews in brief some of the available research evidence about race relations training, with reference to issues raised in the Scarman report. Police race relations training is a hybrid field, drawing on work in police-community relations, race relations, and educational psychology, but for present purposes no attempt is made to cover the extensive literature on those subjects. The focus is upon training designed to increase awareness of and sensitivity towards unfamiliar cultures, and to teach skills in dealing with people, especially with people from these cultures. The references do not provide a comprehensive list, the intention being more to illustrate the kind of evidence.

Attitude and awareness training

2.   It is often assumed that the central purpose of race relations training is to make white attitudes towards black people more tolerant and sympathetic. There may be rather more than this to good race relations, but because attitudes can be measured in a quantitative manner, they tend to be used as a yardstick.

3.   Research on the effectiveness of teaching for better inter-racial attitudes provides a mixture of results. One often-quoted study at a college of further education in London, by Miller (1969) showed that attempts to do this, using information, rational argument, or outright persuasion were likely to prove counter-productive. The author suggested that this was because too weak an argument was offered and because the instructor was perceived as an outsider by the trainees. The importance of 'source credibility' has long been accepted by learning theorists examining change attempts. A more recent study by Verma and Bagley (1979) among 14 - 16 year old secondary school pupils concluded, however, that teaching about race relations did tend to have beneficial effects upon inter-racial tolerance, although these effects were not large.

4.   Smith and Willson (1972) compared the effects of 'group process' training in this country in which teachers and parents of ethnic minority children took part in one group, and white and Asian workers took part in another. Only the first group produced attitude and behaviour change, and this was attributed to the facts that it was residential and that its members shared a common motivation and had a clear goal.

5.   One of the best known American training programmes is the 'Racist Re-education' work of Judy Katz (1976). This combines a variety of learning methods including reading, discussion, encounter groups, lectures etc. Students undergo two intensive weekends of training and the results are partly self-assessed and partly assessed by others on the basis of behaviour over a one month period. Both attitudes and behaviour have been found to improve, particularly attitudes.

6.   Teahan (1975) in the United States studied groups of black and white police officers who met over twelve weekly sessions for role playing and interpersonal feedback. Black officers were positively influenced and felt they had better relations with their white colleagues, but whites, although more sensitised to inter-racial issues, showed increased negative feelings towards blacks. Teahan concluded that this was because the whites saw the programme as intended to enhance the position of blacks, and so felt threatened and hostile. Further work suggested that inter-racial animosities were worsened by experience of the job itself.

7.   There is, of course, only value in trying to change attitudes if they are prejudiced in the first place. In the case of police recruits there is some disagreement as to whether this is so. A recently reported study by Colman and Gorman (1981) tested police recruits' attitudes and compared them with civilian controls. This suggested that the police attracts conservative and authoritarian personalities, that training has only a temporarily liberalising effect and that continued police service results in increasingly illiberal, intolerant attitudes towards coloured people. The "police subculture" rather than training was thus blamed for overriding the liberalising effects of training.

8.   This study was submitted as evidence to Lord Scarman, and has received some publicity, but doubts are expressed in some quarters as to its methods. One critic has argued that the police group were more illiberal because they had a lower educational level than the civilian control group. Others query the reliability of the data collection.

9.   The Colman and Gorman results have been noted by the Working Party on Race Relations training at Hendon, along with those of other attitude studies conducted in the early 1970s within the Metropolitan Police. It was concluded that the evidence was that:

-   recruits tended to be authoritarian, anti-black and illiberal,
-   current training can harden prejudice rather than reduce it,
-   recruits became more tough-minded during probation,
-   current training methods can be counter productive, and
-   training only benefited those who began with sympathetic attitudes.

It was therefore suggested that training should start from the assumption that the attitudes of new entrants to the police would be unhelpful.

10.   Some work on probationers' attitudes has been conducted over the past year by Superintendent Butler of the West Midlands Police. Tests have been developed and were administered to probationers on the Initial Courses at Ryton-in-Dunsmore in the Spring of 1981. All recruits completed questionnaires before and after the Initial Course. Prejudice was found to increase slightly between the two tests, though there was little change in perceptions of West Indian and Asian characteristics. However, on both occasions Asians were perceived in a fairly neutral way, and West Indians in a more negative way. A second study was conducted, in the Autumn of 1981. It followed the same pattern, but was also able to take account of the new 'Associated Police Studies' element of the course: some trainees took these lessons, while some still had the old lessons.

Butler's results suggested that again attitudes were little different before and after the course and that, furthermore, this was so whether the old or the new training was received. In two respects this pattern was broken: more recruits believed immigrants worked as hard as white people and fewer recruits believed that immigrants should conform to the "British way of life" after the training as compared with their attitudes before the training. The new element of training might have some positive effect on attitudes but perhaps only in the perception of recruits to Asians. Butler also compared the attitudes, values, perceptions and opinions of recruits with police constables of more than five years service. The findings suggest that constables with five years police experience were consistently more negative towards ethnic minorities and particularly towards West Indians as compared with Asians. Attitudes may modify and become less negative with the age of police officers, however.

Skills training

11.   Butler notes that present training emphasises the knowledge and attitudinal aspects of race relations, to the neglect of social skills, and that it is lacking in not seeking to answer such fundamental questions as how to deal with hostile encounters with particular groups. Also, he suggests that training must be seen in the wider context of socialisation into the police role, for it cannot be assumed that attitude changes — or the lack of them — are wholly attributable to the course itself. The formal training experience may contribute, but so may other experiences during the training period, and in the long term training represents only a very small part of the young police officer's experience. A Home Office study in Chapeltown (described below) found very few officers willing to say that training courses had taught them anything about dealing with ethnic minorities, whereas nearly all said that experience had taught them a lot. Most sociological studies of policing deal with the powerful influence of the police organisation and occupational culture in moulding the attitudes of police officers. In particular, the role of the first line supervision — the Sergeant and the Inspector — can be crucial, and this was recognised in Lord Scarman's report. He urged better management training for these officers to enable them better to fulfil the closer supervision of probationers which he also recommended. At least one research proposal is known which seeks to study supervisory styles in more detail among these ranks.

12.   Attitude training, racial awareness training, or self awareness training are only of value to policing if they go together with the learning of effective skills. Awareness training may make the police officer more open to learning and experimenting with such skills and the very fact of having a more open mind may increase the officer's ability to communicate with people. But there will still be a need for more behaviourally oriented learning. This means that training must relate to very specific circumstances and must identify the possible ways of reacting to

such circumstances. The definition of behavioural goals will be very specific, so that what is actually taught cannot derive from American research or from British research in non-police fields.

13. It was in the knowledge that skills training needed specific problems to focus on that in 1981 the Home Office Research and Planning Unit carried out a study in the Chapeltown sub-division of the West Yorkshire Metropolitan Police with the aim of working towards clearer definitions of training goals for probationer training in race relations (Southgate, 1982). The study began from first principles by examining the problems faced by police officers in an ethnic minority area, and the extent to which their present training equipped them to deal with such problems. A combination of questionnaires, interviews, and observation was used to gather data. Officers of all ranks were involved, but with a concentration upon uniformed patrol constables.

14. A number of interesting points emerged from the study:

    — The day-to-day contact between the police and some sections of ethnic minority communities — particularly young West Indians — created hostilities which training might have difficulty in compensating for. Hostile attitudes derived not so much from some inherent prejudice as from actual street experience.

    — Young officers are concerned to make a good impression on their superiors. If those superiors make it clear that hostile attitudes and behaviour towards minorities are not approved of, then police-minority relations are likely to benefit.

    — The impact of training was minimal by comparison with that of socialisation into the work group, and this process can perpetrate hostilities. Young officers may find they have to use derogatory language about black people in order to conform with their colleagues.

    — Police officers are very sceptical about the value of training, but they believe strongly in learning by experience.

    — Existing training in race relations was minimal. It was poorly co-ordinated, lacking in agreed goals, and seemed to have little impact. There was little learning of facts, attitudes, or skills. The 'Leeds Scheme' encounter groups between police officers and ethnic minorities were sound in principle, though for the individual police officer they were a short-lived experience. The Scheme could be developed with greater effect.

15. An overall conclusion to be drawn from the study — as with the Butler and Teahan studies quoted earlier — is that the effects of training are difficult to isolate and measure, and may be minor in any case when compared to the effects of learning by experience and absorbing the values of the police occupational culture. The Gorman and Colman study, for example, blamed the occupational culture rather than training for developing illiberal attitudes, and other researchers have also noted the difficulties in distinguishing the effects of training and experience. Is it realistic to hope for any effects at all through training? The answer must be 'yes', but only if training is fully integrated into policing and the police organisation. This means that (a) training and experience must be closely associated, but in a carefully controlled way, (b) training goals and operational goals must coincide, (c) supervisors must reinforce these goals.

16. No one method of training appears to be entirely successful in affecting racial attitudes or awareness. Various types of group work are in favour in management training and human awareness training, though most authorities agree that a variety of methods are needed to supplement each other. Whatever methods are used it seems important for their success that trainees be motivated to learn by seeing benefits to themselves in their everyday working lives. A useful review of methods is provided by Argyle (1981).

Learning on the job. This can be unreliable; a person can do a job for years without discovering the right social skills, or he may learn the wrong skills from his experience. The one great advantage of experience as a training method is that there is no problem of transfer of skills from a training situation to a real-life situation. Close supervision is needed by an experienced practitioner to guide the trainee. This person should give feedback on mistakes being made, demonstrate new methods of behaving, and there must be a good relation between trainee and supervisor.

Reading. This can be useful in combination with more active forms of training. Reading has been found particularly useful in cross-cultural training where there is a lot of information to learn about the rules, ideas, and values of another culture. Programmed texts have been used to prepare people for close contacts with unfamiliar cultures.

Lectures. These can be useful for explaining aspects of skills. Work in management training suggests that lectures may be useful for conveying knowledge, though not for changing attitudes. The impact of lectures can vary greatly depending on the skill of the lecturer.

Group discussions. Their impact again depends greatly on the group leader. They can lead to better assimilation of lecture material and give practice in group behaviour, but are not a good medium for conveying new information.

Films. These can play a part in an overall training scheme, but are of little use alone. They are useful for demonstrating behaviour to trainees.

Training in groups. Argyle is not overly enthusiastic about 'encounter groups' and 'T-groups'. He concludes that the latter can be useful in teaching members about the effect of their behaviour on others and how others see them. In particular, it teaches how to make non-evaluative comments on the behaviour of others.

Role playing. This involves trying out a social skill away from the real-life situation. It is normally preceded by a lecture, discussion, demonstration, or film. A problem situation is then defined and a trained 'stooge' is produced with whom the trainee interacts. This is followed by a feedback session with the trainer and other trainees. Audio and videotapes may be used to record the trainee's performance and be played in the feedback session.

Argyle recommends role playing as a successful form of social skills training. It has, of course, been used in Initial Training Courses for some time and this could be a method of training worth further development, particularly in relation to some of the incidents which cause problems between police and ethnic minorities.

Situational analysis. Argyle suggests that professional training can identify common situations which arise, especially difficult ones, and analyse these with trainees to see what goals, rules, roles etc are involved.

17.   Other work on social skills training has been published from the Ulster Polytechnic and this deals with many of the same types as Argyle. The basic theme of social skills training is the effective management of the verbal and non-verbal aspects of encounters with other people. The Oxford and Ulster work deals mainly with occupations where the helping or persuading of 'clients' is involved. Much of policework falls in these areas, but some does not, and social skills may not always be of great use. The argument in their favour, of course, is that they can reduce the frequency with which interactions cause resentment or degenerate into conflict. A major problem is a lack of systematic documentation of the exact nature of effective policing skills. Some attempts to analyse the minutiae of police-public encounters have been made in America (Sykes and Brent, 1980) but one of the most potentially valuable research projects in this country would be an extensive observational study of police contacts with ethnic minorities. This could throw further light on both what goes wrong and on what goes right.

Summary

18.   There is, unfortunately, no research evidence to fully answer the specific question as to what, if any, is the effect of race relations training given to police officers in Britain. The main reasons for this are that the criteria for measurement are so elusive and are so closely interwoven with other aspects of policing. There is no clear agreement as to what the goals are, except at

more general levels. There is some confusion as to whether attitudes or skills should be taught. There is some ambiguity as to whether the issues of human relations and race relations are distinct at a practical level. The rather diverse evidence cited suggests a need for some experimentation with approaches developed in related fields, or in other countries, but as yet it is difficult to say what will be most effective. It seems clear that two directions will repay exploration: greater human awareness can be developed in probationers, and the practical skills of human communication can be taught to them.

REFERENCES

ARGYLE, M. (1981). 'Methods of social skills training'. In ARGYLE, M. (ed). *Social Skills and Work.* London: Methuen.

BUTLER, A.J.P. (1982). *Effectiveness of Community and Race Relations Training.* (Unpublished).

BUTLER, A.J.P. (1982). Examination of the Influences of Training and Work Experience on the Attitudes and Perceptions of Police Constables.

COLMAN, A. AND FORMAN, P. (Reported in 'The Times' on 23 September 1981 and submitted in evidence to Lord Scarman).

KATZ, J. (1976). *A Systematic Handbook of Exercises for the Re-education of White People with Respect to Racist Attitudes and Behaviour.* University of Massachuesetts. (Unpublished).

KATZ, J. (1978). *White Awareness – Handbook for Anti-Racism Training.* University of Oklahoma Press – Norman.

MILLER, H. (1969). 'The effectiveness of teaching techniques for reducing colour prejudice'. *Liberal Education,* 16: 25-31.

Racism Awareness Training (Pamphlet: available from R.A.P.U., Strand Centre, Lambeth Institute, Elm Park, London SW2).

SMITH, P.B. AND WILSON, M.J. (1972). *A Pilot Investigation to Test the Application of Group Training Methods in the Context of Race Relations.* University of Sussex (Unpublished).

SOUTHGATE, P. (1982). Police Probationer Training in Race Relations. Home Office Research and Planning Unit.

SYKES, R.E. AND BRENT, E.E. (1980). 'The regulation of interaction by police'. Criminology, 18,2: 182-197.

TEAHAN, J.E. (1975). 'Role playing and group experience to facilitate attitude and value changes among black and white police officers', and 'A longitudinal study of attitude shifts among black and white police officers'. *Journal of Social Issues* 31, 1: 35-36.

VERMA, G.K. AND BAGLEY, B. (1979). 'Measured changes in racial attitudes following the use of three different teaching methods'. In *Race, Education and Identity.* London: Macmillan.

Research and Planning Unit
Queen Anne's Gate

OUTLINE SUGGESTED SYLLABUS FOR THE INITIAL TRAINING TO BE GIVEN IN FUTURE TO PROBATIONER CONSTABLES

a. **Constitutional position of the police.** (Lecture and discussion: case studies.)

Short history of the police service; the office of constable — its civilian nature, powers and duties. The framework of accountability — moral as well as legal — to the public. The role of police authorities; the Home Secretary (under the Police Act 1964); post Scarman consultative groups; elected representatives and statutory bodies etc. Accountability at constable level — the "consumer" dimension to police work.

b. **The Ethics of Policing.** (Lecture and discussion)

Concept of professional ethic or code of conduct (cf. doctors, journalists etc). Constable's oath. The meaning of 'consent'. Social needs vs rights of the individual. The right of individuals to equal respect regardless of race, class etc and to equal treatment before the law. The need for professional detachment.

c. **The job of police officer.** (Lecture and discussion: case studies and other factual material.)

Duties as usually described; the protection of life and property; the maintenance of order; the prevention of crime; and the prosecution of offenders. The primacy of keeping the peace and the dilemmas inherent in police work. The need for, and proper exercise of, discretion. The "social work" dimension of police work — the multifarious roles filled by police officers. The need for officers to recognise these "non-operational" roles as part of their jobs and to discharge them satisfactorily.

d. **The operational importance of good community relations.** (Lecture and discussion: case studies — eg. typical CID investigation, and factual presentations.)

Police dependency on public support both in dealing with offences as they arise and preventing crime in the long term. Consequential need to keep public support. The importance of other agencies (eg. social services, probation, CRC's) and the need to liaise with them. The deleterious effect of individual failings on the service as a whole and the need to be aware of the community relations aspect of all police work. Effective policing more than "getting results".

e. **Crime and its associated factors.** (Lecture and discussion: factual presentations.)

Recorded crime and the "dark figure". Most crime relatively trivial. Serious crime still rare. Factors associated with crime especially in inner-city areas. Vast majority even in high-crime areas not criminal. Importance of not stereo-typing people living in high-crime areas. High crime areas also areas with high demand for police services other than law enforcement. Importance of sensitivity in following up crime with victims. Racial attacks.

f. **Importance of adapting policing methods to different localities.** (Lecture and discussion: case studies etc.)

Britain never homogeneous. Now multi-ethnic, multi-cultural. Different areas have different crime profiles, physical and social features. Policing has always adapted to these differences; necessary if policing is to be effective. Equal treatment not equivalent to same treatment.

g. **Race relations.** (Lecture and discussion)

Key position of police as influence for good or bad. The special factors affecting race in contrast to community relations. Moral, social and operational need for good race relations. Need for impeccable professional behaviour. Difficulties between police and minority ethnic groups *as seen from both sides*. The nature of individual and institutional prejudice, and of stereotyping and the dangers of these for the police service and society.

The need for officers to be aware of their effect on others and others' perceptions of them. The evils of racist epithets.

Race relations (ii). (Lecture, discussion, practical exercises and/or films)

Where the police, as an institution, stand on the question of race. Indicate to police officers at the outset of their careers, by way of "setting the tone", that racialist conduct, epithets and so on were unacceptable. The need to make it clear at an early stage to recruits that the highest standards were required in their dealings with minority ethnic groups. Introduction to some of the more testing situations police officers might meet later when they went out onto the streets for the first time.

RACISM AWARENESS PROGRAMME UNIT (RAPU)

1.   One of our members, Ms Dorothy Kuya, is a member of the Racism Awareness Programme Unit (RAPU). RAPU took as its starting point the ideas put forward by Judy H Katz in her book "White Awareness: Handbook for Anti Racism Training." RAPU has developed a programme of training from this base and has found an increasing number of organisations and local services interested in their officers receiving some of the racial awareness training they offer. Their approach and their programme are sketched out below.

Racism: defining the problem

2.   The training offered by RAPU is based on three working assumptions:

   (i)   Britain is a multi-racial society

   (ii)   British society is permeated by racism

   (iii)   Racism in Britain is a white problem.

Tackling the problem

3.   RAPU's approach is to run "workshops" and to create an informal atmosphere where participants can be open and honest about the influence of racism in their lives and work and how they may think or act in a racist way.

The RAPU programme

(i)   **content** The content of the training offered varied according to the background and needs of each group but generally covered the following broad areas:

   Influences on racist thinking and practice: this seeks to demonstrate the way in which history and social influences condition the individuals' perception of race.

   The terms and the language: this explores some of the issues in a preliminary way through discussions of how key terms might best be defined.

   Personal, institutional and cultural racism: this seeks to impart an understanding of the different forms of racism.

   White awareness: this seeks to help develop in white people an awareness of their own racial identity. While ethnic minorities are commonly seen, and see themselves, as a separate group with their own identity, the majority white population rarely perceives itself as a distinctive ethnic and racial group. This area of the course is also designed to explore the difference between how individuals view themselves and how they are seen by others. Courses naturally vary according to the racial composition of the group.

(ii)   **method** Participants are divided into small workshop groups and a variety of methods are used: talks; group discussions; slides and films supported by full discussions, including debriefing sessions; and role play and role reversal exercises including structured group games. Special emphasis is placed on sharing information and experience in group discussion of workable definitions of key concepts (eg discrimination); participants' fears about the course; and the risks attached to them as individuals making a stand against racism as it affects them.

(iii)   **aim** The common aim of the elements in the programme is to clarify for individuals their actions and attitudes and how they might be affected, sometimes unconciously, by race or racism.